# WRESTLING
## FOR FUN!

by Eric Murray

*Content Adviser: Gary Abbot, Former Wrestler, Colorado Springs, Colorado*
*Reading Adviser: Frances J. Bonacci, Ed.D., Reading Specialist, Cambridge, Massachusetts*

## COMPASS POINT BOOKS
### MINNEAPOLIS, MINNESOTA

Compass Point Books
3109 West 50th street, #115
Minneapolis, MN 55410

Visit Compass Point Books on the Internet at www.compasspointbooks.com
or e-mail your request to custserv@compasspointbooks.com

Photographs ©: Comstock Klips, front cover (left), 14; Rubberball Productions, front cover (right), 10-11, 14-15, 15, 16-17, 47; AJ Mast/Icon SMI, 5; Photodisc, 6-7, 43, 44, 45; AP Wide World Photos, 8-9, 20-21, 26-27, 31, 32, 34-35, 38-39, 40, 41; AJ Mast/Icon SMI, 12-13, 25; Li we hb/Imaginechina/Icon SMI, 19, 22–23; Mark Cowan/Icon SMI, 28-29; Corel, 33, 42-43; Crosnier/DPPI-SIPA/Icon SMI, 36-37.

Editors: Deb Berry and Aubrey Whitten/Bill SMITH STUDIO; and Shelly Lyons
Designer/Page Production: Geron Hoy, Kavita Ramchandran, Sinae Sohn, Marina Terletsky, and Brock Waldron/Bill SMITH STUDIO
Photo Researcher: Jacqueline Lissy Brustein, Scott Rosen, and Allison Smith/Bill SMITH STUDIO
 Art Director: Jaime Martens
Creative Director: Keith Griffin
Editorial Director: Carol Jones
Managing Editor: Catherine Neitge

**Library of Congress Cataloging-in-Publication Data**
Murray, Eric.
 Wrestling for fun! / by Eric Murray.
    p. cm. — (For fun!)
 Includes bibliographical references and index.
 ISBN 0-7565-1687-0 (hard cover)
 1. Wrestling—Juvenile literature.  I. Title. II. Series.
 GV1195.3.M87 2005
 796.812—dc22
                              2005030733

Printed in the United States of America.

# Table of Contents

## The Ground Rules

## Playing the Game

## People, Places, and Fun

Note: In this book, there are two kinds of vocabulary words. Wrestling Words to Know are words specific to wrestling. They are defined on page 46. Other Words to Know are helpful words that aren't related only to wrestling. They are defined on page 47.

# An Age-Old Sport

**H**ave you ever seen a wrestling match? Wrestling is an exciting sport that grows more popular every year. In fact, people have been competing in wrestling matches for thousands of years, making it one of the oldest sports in the world.

The first evidence of wrestling can be traced back almost 5,000 years to Middle Eastern works of art. Illustrations of wrestling techniques that are still in use today can be seen on Egyptian drawings dating back to 2500 B.C.

The first modern Olympics, in 1896, featured wrestling to provide a link to the Olympic games of the distant past. Wrestling is still a part of the Olympics today.

There are many forms of wrestling, but they all have one thing in common: two opponents pitting their strength and skill against each other to see who is the best.

# Inside the Ring

**S**een from above, a wrestling mat looks a lot like an archery target, except it's much larger. The size of the mat depends on whether the match is a high school, college, or international contest.

A standard high school mat is 38 feet (12 meters) long and wide, with a 10-foot (3-m) diameter circle in the middle. That ring is the central surface where the action takes place. The very center of the mat has a small rectangle. The area of the mat outside of the larger circle is called the protection area. The color of the mat coincides with the school colors.

As you move up from the high school level, the mats get larger, but the details are similar. Collegiate and International wrestling mats both have central surfaces, protection areas, and corners, but the dimensions can vary based on the level of competition. International wrestling mats have circles in the center, as opposed to the rectangles on high school and college mats.

## Get in There!

Wrestlers are required to be aggressive. Spending too much time in the red, or passive, zone can result in a penalty.

## High School Mat Sizes

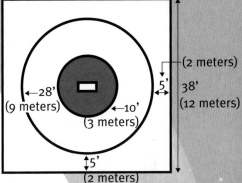

(2 meters)
5'
38'
(12 meters)
28'
(9 meters)
10'
(3 meters)
5'
(2 meters)

## National Collegiate Athletic Association Mat Sizes

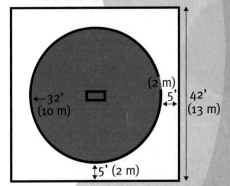

(2 m)
5'
42'
(13 m)
32'
(10 m)
5' (2 m)

## International Mat Sizes

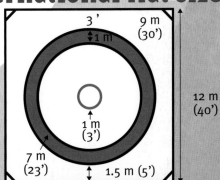

3'
1 m
9 m
(30')
12 m
(40')
1 m
(3')
7 m
(23')
1.5 m (5')

# Opponents in the Circle

**W**restling is for anyone. There is a weight class for just about everybody, regardless of age or gender. A weight class matches up opponents of similar size and ability in order to prevent an unfair advantage, or even injury. You never want to get in the ring with someone who is twice your size!

If you want to get involved with the sport, chances are your school offers wrestling as an after-school activity. If not, check with your local boys' and girls' clubs. Some local organizations hold wrestling camps, which are another great way to get into the sport.

Wrestling has many benefits: You can make new friends, challenge yourself, gain physical fitness and self esteem, and feel the thrill of competition!

# Rules of the Match

**Y**our goal as a wrestler is to take your opponent from a standing position down to the ground, pinning his or her shoulders to the mat. To pin your opponent, once you have taken him or her down to the ground, you must turn your opponent's shoulders toward the mat. If you cannot pin him or her, you can still win the match by scoring the most points.

A wrestling match consists of three two-minute rounds (or periods), with a 30-second break between each period. If a wrestler wins two out of the three periods, he or she wins the match.

If you pin your opponent in any of the three rounds, you win the match.

A tally of points is recorded for each period.

The wrestler with the most points at the end of each two-minute period wins that period.

If a two-minute period ends in a tie, the round is decided by a clinch. A clinch is when both wrestlers take body lock holds. The first wrestler to let go will lose the clinch—and the round. You can also win the clinch, and the round, by scoring a point.

# The Moves

**W**restling matches are scored using a point system. The points you score depend on the moves you make.

### One Point

- a takedown from a standing position to the stomach
- gaining control
- reversal of control
- holding opponent in a danger position (a danger position occurs when a wrestler's back is toward the mat, and either one elbow or one shoulder is in contact with the mat)
- shoulder exposure (occurs when a wrestler's back is toward the mat, but he or she does not have an elbow or shoulder in contact with the mat)

### Two Points

A wrestler can score two points by putting an opponent in or through a danger position.

## Three Points

A wrestler can score three points by taking an opponent from a standing position to a danger position.

## Five Points

A wrestler can score five points by throwing an opponent. In order to score the full five points, a wrestler must:

- throw an opponent above the waist by grabbing him or her slightly above the midsection, causing him or her to lose all contact with the ground

- cause an opponent's body to arc in the air

- cause an opponent's heels to go over his or her head

### Did You Know?

If either wrestler steps into the protection area on the mat, the match is stopped and resumes in the center of the ring.

# Gearing Up for the Match

**W**restling is a very physical sport, but only a few items are required in order to properly equip yourself for a match.

The singlet is the wrestler's uniform. It is a one-piece outfit that is usually made of tight fitting material. The elastic-like fabric allows for easy movement. The tight fit prevents things from getting caught in loose fabric while wrestling an opponent.

Wrestling shoes are lightweight and flexible. The soles are made to grip the surface of the mat in order to give the wrestler the most traction possible.

Since a lot of wrestling moves involve grappling with your opponent while keeping your head down, one of the most important pieces of equipment is the headgear. It fits over your ears and keeps them from being injured.

## Kneepads

Many wrestlers choose to wear kneepads. Kneepads protect your knees from scrapes and bruises. They are especially important if the surface of the wrestling mat is made from a rough material, like canvas.

# Ready, Set, Wrestle!

**B**efore every match, both wrestlers shake hands as a sign of good sportsmanship. The match begins in the neutral position, where both wrestlers face each other in the center of the ring.

The only other starting position during a match is called the referee's position, or *par terre*. The wrestler kneels at the center, with his or her hands 8 inches (20 centimeters) in front of (and in line with) the knees. The wrestler's feet must not be crossed, and the toes must be flat on the mat. This position is used when a wrestler is cautioned for an illegal move or for being too passive.

The match begins when the referee blows the whistle.

# All the Right Moves!

**T**here are four basic moves that earn points during a wrestling match: escapes, reversals, takedowns, and exposure.

**Escape**: An escape occurs when a wrestler breaks free from an opponent's hold, stands up, and faces the opponent.

**Reversal**: A reversal happens when a wrestler breaks free from an opponent's hold and gains a position of control on top of the other wrestler.

**Takedown**: A takedown is when one wrestler takes the other wrestler from a standing position down to the mat.

**Exposure**: Exposure occurs when one wrestler is able to slant an opponent's back past a 90-degree angle toward the mat.

## Toughen Up!

Wrestlers are not allowed to be overly passive or defensive. If a wrestler backs up, circles, or refuses to make contact, he or she may be cautioned for passivity. The match stops, and the offender must resume the match from the referee's position.

# Getting Out of a Bind

**D**uring a match, you may find that your opponent has you locked in a solid hold and is trying to pin you to the mat. Now is the time for an escape!

Here are some escape strategies that wrestlers use:

**Rolls**: The pinned wrestler rolls out from under the wrestler on top, often turning the opponent over and gaining a dominant position. A well-known version of this move is called a Granby roll.

### The Granby Roll

The Granby roll is named for the school where it originated: Granby High School in Norfolk, Virginia.

**Bridge**: To perform a bridge, arch your back when you are in danger of being pinned to the mat. This can help you to gain enough leverage to get out from under your opponent.

**Sitout**: A sitout is an escape where the wrestler swings his or her legs out from beneath an opponent, moves into a sitting position, and then rolls over with the outside leg. This gives the wrestler a strong base from which to push off the opponent and continue the match.

# That's Not Allowed!

Illegal holds are dangerous and can cause injury. Whenever a referee witnesses one of these holds being used, he awards one point to the offender's opponent. Illegal holds include, but are not limited to:

**Slam**: The wrestler lifts and returns an opponent to the mat with excessive force.

**Hammerlock**: The wrestler pulls the opponent's arms too high on the back or pulls the arm away from the back.

**Headlock**: The wrestler's arms or hands are locked around an opponent's head without encircling an arm.

**Full Nelson**: The wrestler's arms are under both arms and behind the head of his or her opponent.

# Calling the Shots

**A** wrestling match would go on forever if there weren't a person there to score points and declare a winner. A referee watches closely for points scored, falls, pins, or illegal moves. He or she assigns points and penalties based on the official rules, and is the person in charge of everything that happens on the wrestling mat.

In major wrestling events, there are three officials for a wrestling match:

**Referee**: The official who is on the mat with the competitors.

**Judge**: A second official who watches the match from a spot off of the mat.

**Chairman**: A third official who resolves disagreements between the referee and the judge.

# Stay Protected!

**W**restling is fun and exciting, but you should always make sure to take the necessary precautions to protect yourself from serious injury.

Never wrestle anyone who is outside of your weight class. If an opponent is bigger than you, you could be seriously injured.

If you wrestle someone who is much smaller than you are, you could hurt your opponent just by applying normal wrestling moves.

Always pay attention to what your wrestling coach teaches you about proper technique and how to avoid illegal moves. Also be aware of incorrect holds that can cause injury to others.

# Whatever You Say, Coach!

**O**nce you decide to get started in wrestling, the most important person you'll have on your side will be your coach. He or she will act as your guide and trainer.

It's important to remember that your coach wants you to win but is also looking out for your best interests. He or she can provide advice on technique and training that will make you a better athlete.

Your coach has a responsibility to help you develop your skills as a wrestler. He or she should also guide you in maintaining honor as a competitor. A good coach would never suggest training methods that are improper or wrestling conduct that is unsportsmanlike.

# Put Your Opponent Away

**Y**ou've used your best moves, and your opponent has put some pretty good moves on you, but the match can't go on forever. The first wrestler to win two out of three periods will be the winner. Here's what has to happen in order to win the match:

**Win by Points**: A wrestling match can be won when one opponent scores more points than the other by the end of the allotted time. Points are awarded throughout the match by the referee.

**Pin**: Pinning the opponent is the ultimate goal of the match. A pin occurs when a wrestler holds both of the opponent's shoulders to the mat for a certain amount of time. Remember: *Pinning is winning!*

**Forfeit**: A forfeit happens when an opponent suffers an injury and cannot continue, is disqualified for unsportsmanlike conduct, or fails to show up for the match. It is the least desirable way to win a match, but it does count.

# Sumo and *Lucha Libre*

**I**n Mexico, popular wrestling is called *lucha libre* or "free wrestling." The wrestlers wear colorful masks and capes. The mask is so much a part of a wrestler's identity that some wear them all the time, wherever they go!

Some wrestlers have had their identities passed down to them from their fathers. One of the more popular wrestlers in the 1960s was named Santo. He was so popular that he even starred in many Mexican films. When he grew too old to continue, his son took over the role, and Santo continued to be the most popular *luchador* (fighter) in Mexico.

The Japanese form of wrestling is called *sumo*. It is an ancient form of wrestling that is based on a strict lifestyle and rules of honor. Sumo wrestlers are distinguished by their large size and traditional Japanese clothing. Sumo wrestlers commit to this lifestyle until they retire and are revered in Japan as heroes.

The first non-Japanese sumo wrestler to become a champion was Salevaa Atisanoe, whose sumo name was Konishiki. He was born in Hawaii and entered sumo in 1982. Konishiki rose to the top-most division in two years. Three years later he reached the rank of *ozeki*, or "champion." Konishiki retired in 1997 with one of the best records in sumo history.

# Ladies Only!

**U**ntil recently, it was difficult for girls and women to get involved in the sport of wrestling. The first females to break into the sport had to wrestle against male opponents, but their determination paved the way for other girls and women to gain access to a proud and competitive sport.

Women's freestyle wrestling is growing around the world. A world championship for women was created in the 1980s. Since 1989, the United States has been participating in the Women's Freestyle World Championships. In July 1997, the U.S. team placed third in the team competition and produced three silver medalists.

The growing popularity of women's wrestling was reflected in the fact that it was the only new sport to be included in the 2004 Summer Olympic Games in Athens, Greece.

# Carry the Torch

**T**he Olympic Games is where wrestling gets the most exposure and attention. For anyone heavily involved in competitive wrestling, qualifying to represent your country in the Olympics is often the ultimate goal. Imagine working hard enough to become one of the best in your country, and then going on to compete against the best wrestlers in the rest of the world!

Some athletes train for years for a chance to represent their country. The pressure and sacrifice that go into training for the Olympics can wear down all but the most strong-willed competitor. To be an Olympic champion, you must have a mind that is as strong as your body. Anyone who has ever had a gold medal draped around his or her neck will tell you it was worth every ounce of effort.

# Faking It for the Fans!

**P**rofessional wrestling is scripted entertainment, much like a live theater performance. It does not involve competitive matches. Its colorful cast of characters, heroes and villains, act out intense rivalries with amazing acrobatic moves.

Some professional wrestlers got their start in competitive wrestling. In fact, pro wrestler Kurt Angle was a gold medal-winning freestyle wrestler in the 100-kilogram (220-pound) freestyle wrestling competition at the 1996 Olympic Games in Atlanta. He won even though he had two fractured vertebrae in his neck!

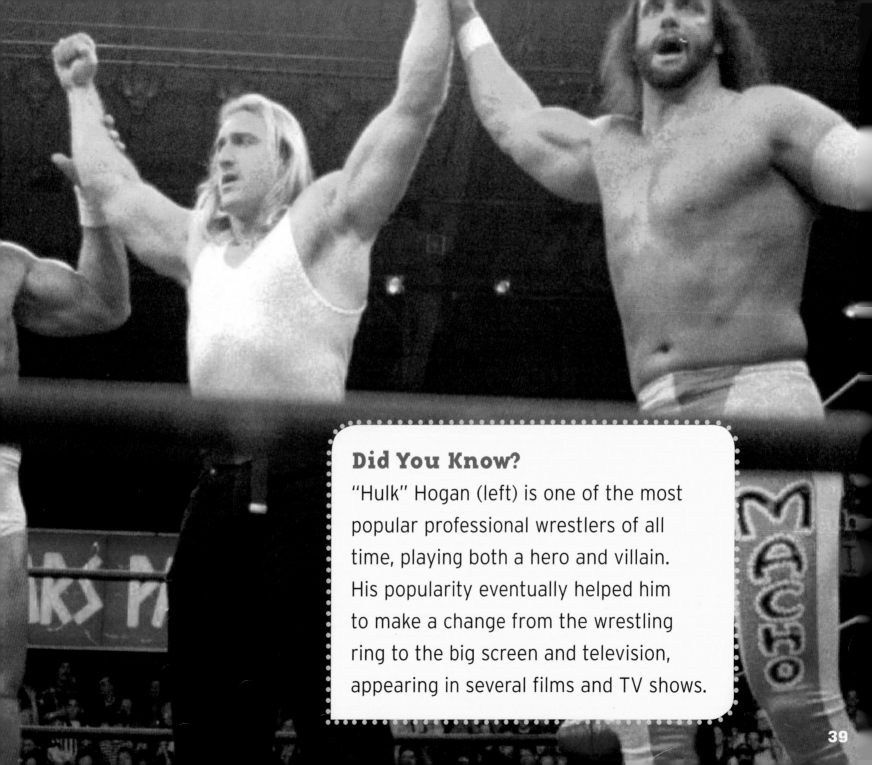

**Did You Know?**

"Hulk" Hogan (left) is one of the most popular professional wrestlers of all time, playing both a hero and villain. His popularity eventually helped him to make a change from the wrestling ring to the big screen and television, appearing in several films and TV shows.

# Who's Who in Wrestling

### DAN GABLE (U.S.)

Dan Gable won the gold medal at 149 pounds (67 kg) at the 1972 Summer Olympics, despite a painful shoulder injury. In fact, Gable did not surrender a single point at the 1972 Games. Gable had a combined 182-1 record in high school and at Iowa State University. As a coach for the Iowa Hawkeyes, he led his team to 15 national titles. He was the head coach of the U.S. Olympic team in freestyle wrestling in 1984 and 2000.

Dan Gable

Alexander Karelin

Rulon Gardner

## ALEXANDER KARELIN (SOVIET UNION AND RUSSIA)

Alexander Karelin was a dominant Greco-Roman wrestler for the Soviet Union and later for Russia. He won gold medals at the 1988, 1992, and 1996 Olympic Games.

Nicknamed the "Russian Dan Gable," he went undefeated in international competition from 1987 until 2000, when he was upset by American Rulon Gardner in the gold medal match at the Summer Olympics. Karelin went the last six years of his unbeaten streak without giving up a point.

# What Happened When?

1880     1910     1920     1930     1960     1970

**1888** The first organized Amateur Athletic Union (AAU) National Tournament is held in New York City.

**1921** The first high school state tournament is held in Ames, Iowa.

**1961** The first World Championships in which the United States competes are held in Japan. The U.S. freestyle and Greco-Roman teams both finish sixth.

**1896** The first Olympic Games of the modern era are held in Athens, Greece, with nine sports, including wrestling.

**1928** The first NCAA wrestling tournament is held in Ames, Iowa.

**1969** Rick Sanders and Fred Fozzard become the first Americans to win world freestyle titles.

**1908** Iowan Frank Gotch defeats Russian-trained George Hackenschmidt for the world heavyweight professional title in Chicago, setting off a wrestling boom in the United States.

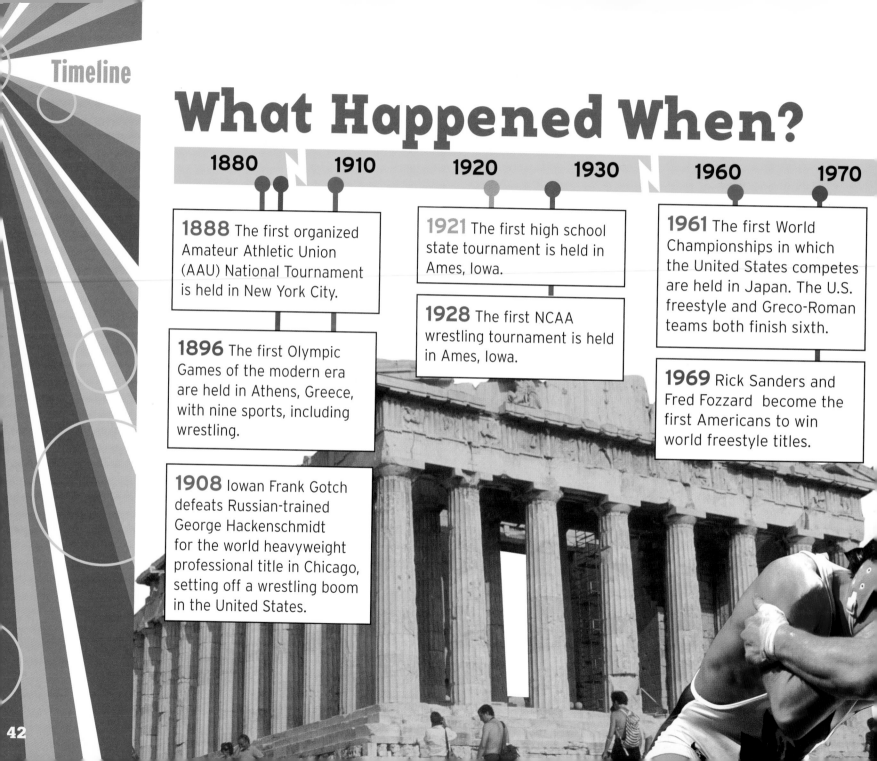

Toronto, Canada

| 1970 | 1975 | 1980 | 1985 | 1990 | 1995 | 2000 |

**1971** The Junior National Championships, now run by USA Wrestling and considered to be the largest wrestling tournament in the world, are held for the first time in Iowa City, Iowa.

**1972** Dan Gable and Wayne Wells win Olympic gold medals, becoming the first U.S. wrestlers to win two world titles.

**1983** USA Wrestling becomes the national governing body for amateur wrestling in the United States.

**1984** The United States wins its first wrestling medals in modern Greco-Roman Olympic competitions.

**1986** USA Wrestling is formally recognized by Fédération Internationnal des Luttes Associées (FILA), the international governing body for wrestling, as a permanent representative.

**1987** John Smith of Oklahoma State wins the the first of six straight world freestyle titles.

**1990** Wrestler John Smith wins the Sullivan Award, given each year to the outstanding amateur athlete.

**1993** The United States wins its first-ever World Team Title in Toronto, Canada.

**2004** Cael Sanderson, from Herber, Utah, wins a gold medal in the men's freestyle 84 kg (185 pound) wrestling competition at the 2004 Olympic Games in Athens, Greece.

# Fun Wrestling Facts

Wrestling became an Olympic sport in 708 B.C. It was also the final and decisive event of the Pentathalon–a five event combination of discus, javelin, jumping, running, and wrestling.

The United States won every gold medal in wrestling during the 1904 Olympic Games. The United States was the only nation that entered a team in the Olympic competition that year.

Former U.S. presidents George Washington, Abraham Lincoln, and Teddy Roosevelt all participated in the sport of wrestling.

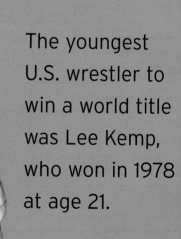

The youngest U.S. wrestler to win a world title was Lee Kemp, who won in 1978 at age 21.

Swing dancing takes its name from a form of wrestling that was popular in Switzerland in the 1940s.

The Wrestling Hall of Fame is located in Stillwater, Oklahoma. It opened in 1974.

The first female amateur high school match took place on December 10, 1987, in Fort Lauderdale, Florida.

The longest Olympic wrestling contest ever was the 1912 semifinal bout between Martin Klein of Russia and Alfred Asikainen of Finland. The match lasted 11 hours.

# Wrestling Words to Know

**aggressiveness:** a characteristic possessed by good wrestlers that enables them to be consistently on the attack

**body lock:** a move in which the wrestler locks his or her arms around an opponent's torso and attempts to throw him or her to the mat

**caution:** a penalty for using an illegal hold or when a defensive wrestler deliberately leaves the mat to avoid being scored upon

**decision:** awarded to the wrestler who has earned the greater number of points

**default:** awarded when one of the competitors is unable to continue wrestling for any reason

**escape:** moving from the bottom position to the neutral position

**exposure:** when a wrestler is angled backward and his or her back is facing the mat

**fall:** pinning the opponent's shoulders to the mat

**forfeit:** awarded to a wrestler when his or her opponent suffers an injury and cannot continue, is disqualified for unsportsmanlike conduct, or fails to show up for the match

**neutral position:** a position in which neither wrestler has control; the wrestlers are both on their feet, opposite each other

**passivity:** when the officials believe that one wrestler is not wrestling actively enough

**period:** one of the three lengths of time that make up a wrestling match

**pin:** forcing both of an opponent's shoulder blades onto the mat

**reversal:** a maneuver in which a competitor being controlled by the opponent suddenly reverses the situation and gains control

**singlet:** a collarless undergarment for the body

**takedown:** occurs when from standing, one wrestler takes his or her opponent to the mat

**throw:** an attempt to gain a takedown and points for putting the opponent's back to the mat in one maneuver

**tilt (or Danger Position):** when the wrestler turns his or her opponent so the opponent's shoulders face the mat at an angle of less than 90 degrees

**weight class:** a system that divides wrestlers of similar weight into evenly matched groups

# Other Words to Know

**amateur:** a person who engages in an activity as a pastime, not a job

**maneuver:** movement or action that requires skill or dexterity

**precaution:** things done before an event to prevent harm

**sportsmanship:** the practice of fair play, courtesy, and grace in winning or losing

## Where To Learn More

### AT THE LIBRARY

Jarman, Tom, and Reid Hanley. *Wrestling for Beginners*. Chicago, Ill: Contemporary Books, 1983.

Mysnyk, Mark, Barry Davis, and Brooks Simpson. *Winning Wrestling Moves*. Champaign, Ill: Human Kinetics Publishers, 1994.

American Sport Education Program. *Coaching Youth Wrestling*. Champaign, Ill: Human Kinetics Publishers, 2001.

### ON THE ROAD

National Wrestling Hall of Fame and Museum
405 W. Hall of Fame
Stillwater, OK 74075
405/377-5243

### ON THE WEB

For more information on this topic, use FactHound.

1. Go to *www.facthound.com*
2. Type in this book ID: 0756516870
3. Click on the *Fetch It* button.

FactHound will find the best Web sites for you.

# INDEX

## ABOUT THE AUTHOR

Eric Murray is a writer who lives in Jersey City, New Jersey. In addition to being a writer, he is also an avid musician and graphic artist.